IRISH
TUNES
for
PIANO

Published by permission from Kerr's Music Corporation, Glasgow

Lay-out and Design by John Loesberg

Ossian Publications Ltd. Ireland
(Publishing Dept.)
P.O.Box, Cork

Ossian Publications Scotland
9 Rosebery Crescent
Edinburgh EH12 5JP

Ossian Publications U.K.
Unit 3, Prince William Rd
Loughborough, Leics. LE11 0GU

Ossian Publications USA
RR8 Box 374
Loudon, New Hampshire
03301

OMB73
ISBN 0 946005 78 8

Printed by Watermans, Cork

Irish Tunes for Piano

The Rakes of Kildare.

Arr. by A.E. Moffat

Dear harp of my Country.

"New Langolee."

The Foggy Dew.

From Bunting's Collection, 1840.

Limerick Air.

From Dr. Joyce's Collection.

O hark and leave this sacred isle.

"The Brown Thorn."

The Cruiskeen Lawn.

Limerick Dance Tune.

D.C.

4

Adieu, lovely Mary.

No, not more welcome.

"Luggelaw."

Ballad Air.

Andante.

From the Petrie Collection.

Nay, tell me not, dear.

Moderato.

"Dennis, don't be threatening."

Jackson's Morning Brush.

Composed by Jackson, *circa* 1760.

Allegretto vivo.

Mr. Jackson's Hornpipe.

Vivace.

Has sorrow thy young days shaded.

"Sly Patrick."

Molto Andante.

Come o'er the sea.

"Cuishla ma chree."

Andantino.

The captivating youth.

The Girl I left behind me.

She is far from the Land.

"Open the door."

Remember Thee.

"Castle Tirowen".

Shule Arun.

Oh! blame not the bard.

"Kitty Tyrrell."

The Irish Hautboy.

The Basket of oysters.

Jackson's Favorite.

Silent, O Moyle!

"Arah, my dear Ev'len".

The Humours of Glyn.

Allegretto quasi Andantino.

Green woods of Truicha.

Andante espressivo.

From Mulholland's Collection, 1810.

Fairest Creature.

From Mulholland's Collection, 1810.

Andante molto.

To Ladies eyes.

"Faque a Ballagh".

Spiritoso.

D.C. al Fine.

O' Connor's Lament.

Oh, for the swords of former times!

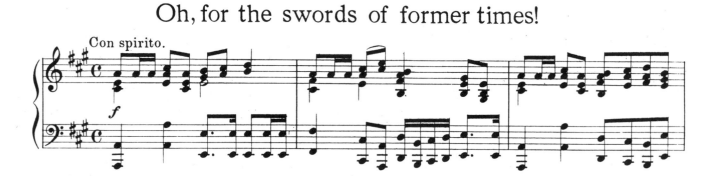

Kissing and drinking.

Peggy Bawne's Jig.

From O'Farrell's Collection, *circa* 1800.

The Shan van Voght.
(The poor old woman.)

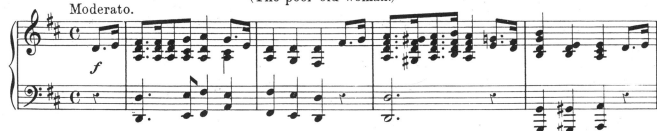

Mountains High.

Andantino.

From Mulholland's Collection, 1810.

I'd mourn the hopes that leave me.

"The Irish Lilt"
"The gimlet"
"The Rose tree" etc.

Allegretto con grazia.

My Bonny Cuckoo.

Andantino.

Cradle Song.

From Dr. Joyce's Collection.

If thou'lt be mine.

"The winnowing sheet."

There are sounds of mirth.

"The Priest in his Boots."

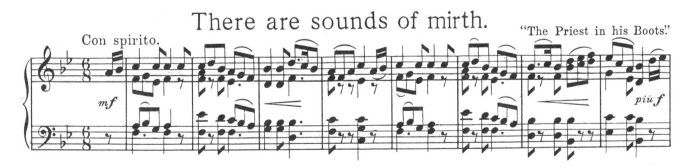

The Young May Moon.

Allegretto.

"The Dandy O."

Silence is in our festal halls.

Largo.

"The green woods of Truigha."

Little brother of my heart.

Coola Shore.

Joyce's Lament.

Kitty O' Toole.

I've a secret to tell thee.

"Oh, Southern Breeze."

The Swaggering Jig.

"Oh! for the marriage."

The Flower of Donnybrook.

Vivace.   Reel.

The Kerry Jig.

Con spirito.   From Holden's Collection. c. 1800.

Pretty Mistress Hannah.

Allegro.

Limerick Air.

From the Petrie Collection.

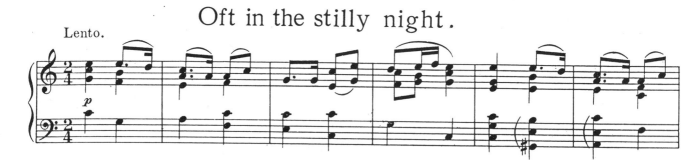

Oft in the stilly night.

It's a pity I don't see my love.

Kitty Magee.

Widow Machree.

Composed by Samuel Lover.

The Legacy.

Andantino.

The last Rose of Summer.

Andante espressivo.

"The young man's dream."
"The groves of Blarney."
"Castle Hyde."

The Meeting of the Waters.

Poco andante.

"The old Head of Denis."

The Honourable Thomas Burk.

Composed by Carolan.

Allegretto.

Captain Macdonald's Favorite Jig.

Con spirito.

From O'Farrell's Coll. 1810.

The Widow Dickens.

Spiritoso.

Farewell! – but whenever you welcome the hour.

Poco andante.

"Moll Roone."

Here we dwell.

Moderato.

"Cean dubh deelish."

Stepney's Rant.

Carolan's Cup.

Daniel the worthy.

Paddy O'Rafferty.

Little Molly, O.

Daniel's Dream.

Cossey's Jig.

Composed by Jackson, c. 1760.

Judy you flirt.

Allegretto.

'Twas one of those Dreams.

Andante espressivo.

"The Song of the Woods."

Weep on.

Andante.

"The Song of Sorrow."

Two Mile Bridge.

Paddy O'Carrol.

Paddy Whack.

Fill the bumper fair.

"Bob and Joan".

Do you remember that night?

Far beyond yon Mountains.

From the Petrie Collection.

The Rejected Lover.

"An Graidheair duilteach".

The Washerwoman.

Abigail Judge.

Composed by Carolan.

Mrs. Trench.

Composed by Carolan.

My Gentle Harp.

"The Coina."

Rich and rare were the gems she wore.

Andantino.

"The Summer is coming."

Love's Young Dream.

Allegretto con grazia.

"The Old Woman."

The Bells of Shandon.

Andante molto.

"The Groves of Blarney".

The Fair Black-haired little Rose.

Andante.

"Rois gael Dubh".

Forget not the field.

Lento molto espressione.

"The Lamentation of Aughrim".

Patrick's Pot.

Did you hear of the Widow Malone.

Come, rest on this bosom.

Saint Patrick's Day.

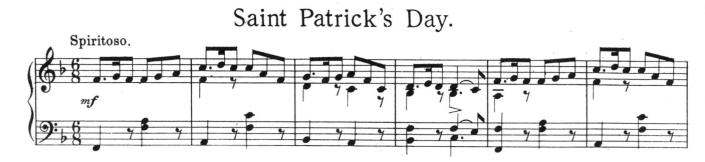

The Fairy Rath.

The Rakes of Frishmen.

The Pullet.

Hornpipe.

The Mountains of Wicklow.

Jig.

Irish Lilt.

The Pretty girl milking the cow.

Jig to the Irish Cry.

From Burk Thumoth's Collection, ca. 1740.

Diarmid ua Duda.

The Minstrel Boy.

"The Moreen".

Ballygarvie.

Drum.

Composed by Jackson, circa 1760.

Off she goes.

Composed by Jackson, *circa* 1760.

The Whigsborough Hunt.

Who'll come fight in the snow.

She is a lovely girl.

My heart is heavy.

Lament.

From Dr. P. W. Joyce's Collection.

The Bucks of Westmeath.

From Holden's Collection, c. 1800.

Limerick Lasses.

The Harp that once thro' Tara's Halls.

"Gramachree".

Andante.

The Flannel Jacket.

From Petrie's Collection Vol. II.

Vivace.

Jig.

Con spirito.

The unfortunate cup of tea.

Reel.

Vivace.

Planxty Connor.

From Carolan's Collection of Irish Tunes.

Con energia.

The Lovely Derry Air

Andante espressivo.

From Petrie's Collection.

While gazing on the moon's light.

"Oonagh".

Poco andante.

Little Donnell.

"Donnal Og."

Adagio con espressione.

One bumper at parting.

"Moll Roe."

Allegro moderato.

The Sprig of Shillelah.

The top of Cork Road.

"The Yorkshire Lasses".

Ballinderry.

The time I've lost in wooing.

The Lake of Coolfin.

O! had we some bright little Isle.

"Sheelah na Guira."

Allegretto.

The Barley Grain.

Con spirito.

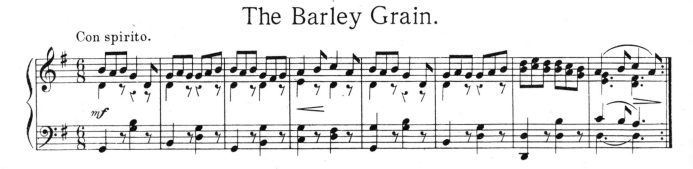

The yellow Flail.

"An suiste Buidhe."

The Winter it is past.

Dr. Petrie's version.

Did you hear of Boccough.

From "The Beggar's Wedding" 1729.

Kennedy's Jig.

The pretty lasses of Loughrea.

Rowdledum.

The Farmer's Lament.

Andante quasi adagio.

From O'Farrell's Collection, c. 1810.

Crotty's Lament.

Andante espressivo.

From O'Farrell's "Pocket Companion."

The Black Rock.

Allegretto.

From O'Farrell's Collection.

Wellington's coming.

By O'Farrell's Collection, *circa*. 1810.

Remember the glories of Brien the brave.

"Molly Macalpin."

The little house under the hill.

Barney Brallaghan's Courtship.

"Blewitt's Jig."

The Peacock.

Wreathe the bowl.

"Nora Kista."

Allegretto spiritoso.

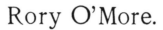

Rory O'More.

Con spirito.

The Summer is come and the grass is green.

From Dr. P. W. Joyce's Collection.

Adagio espressivo.

Single Jig.

Con spirito.

Reel.

Allegro vivace.

King Charles' Jig.

Spiritoso.

Along with my love I'll go.

Mulholland's version.

Lento.

No surrender.

Allegro moderato.

The Blooming Meadows.

Spiritoso.

Saint Patrick was a gentleman.

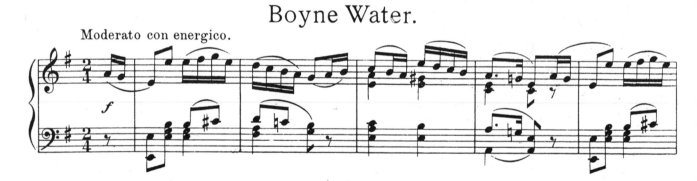

Boyne Water.

Barndoor Jig.

The Fairy King's Courtship.

From Dr. P. W. Joyce's Collection.

Fly not yet.

"Planxty Kelly."

Peggy Bawn.

Moderato.

p

cresc. con espress.

p

rit.

Desmond's Song.

Andante molto maestoso.

mf

f

rit.

Fairest! put on awhile.

Poco allegretto.

"Cummilium."

p

con Ped.

Lesbia hath a beaming eye.

"Nora Creina."

Mabel Kelly.

Oh! Arranmore.

Adagio con espressiono.

I saw from the beach.

Moderato.

The Bottle of Punch.

Allegro spiritoso.

Jack in the green.

Have you been at Carrick?

From Dr. Joyce's Collection.

Paddy's Return.

Reel.

From O'Farrell's Coll. *circa* 1810.

Go to the devil and shake yourself.

The Strawberry Blossom.

Reel.

The Humours of Limerick.

Allegro moderato.

The Rakes of Clonmel.

Allegro moderato.

How sweet the answer Echo makes.

Drolien, or "The Wren"

I've a secret to tell thee.

"Oh, Southern Breeze."

Erin! the tear and the smile in thine eyes.

"Aileen-a-Roon."

*Suantraidhe.
Nurse-Song, or Lullaby.

Andante espressivo.

The Rakes of Mallow.

From Burk Thumoth's Collection.

Spiritoso.

Miss Brady.
Reel.

Allegro.

*Pronounced Soontree.

The Wearing of the Green.

Andante espressivo.

W. E. Hudson's version. 1841.

As a beam on the Waters.

Andante molto.

"The young man's dream."

Avenging and bright.

"Cruachan na Feinne."

Allegro moderato e con energia.

Burke's Jig.

Allegro molto.

Go where glory waits thee.

"The Maid of the Valley."

Molto andante e maestoso.

Let Erin remember.

"The Red Fox."

Oh! Love is a hunter boy.

"The Gentle Maiden."

Moll in the Wad.

Oh! breathe not his name.

"The Brown Maid."

"Tho' the last glimpse of Erin."

"The Coolun."

Dublin Streets.

Allegro molto.

Irish War Song.

Molto maestoso.

The Merchant's Daughter."

The Low-backed car.

"Jack the jolly ploughboy."

Con spirito.

Kitty of Coleraine.

"Paddy's Resource."

Allegretto.

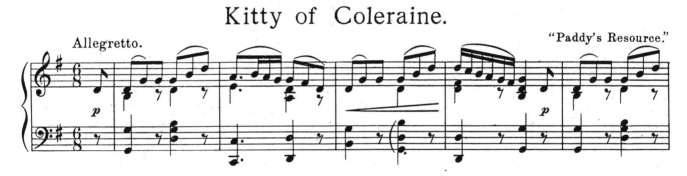

The Humours of Mullin-a-Faunia.

How dear to me.

Mr. Walker's Hornpipe.

Kate Kearney.

"The Beardless Boy."

Poco Allegretto.

Lilleburlero.

Moderato.

Also known as "The Protestant Boys."

'Tis believed that this harp.

"Gage Fane."

Andante.

Garryowen.

Barney O'Hea.

Samuel Lover.

Ossian Publications
Publishers & Distributors of Irish & General Music in
Print and on Audio Tape

Ossian Publications produce a large range of Irish and
other music for traditional & classical instruments,
music cassettes as well as collections of songs, tunes,
instruction books and items on the history of Irish
music.

For our complete list, send us an (international) postal
reply coupon and your name and address.

Ossian Publications, P.O.Box 84
Cork, Ireland